W9-AJP-873

J
1.5
War

RHODE
ISLAND

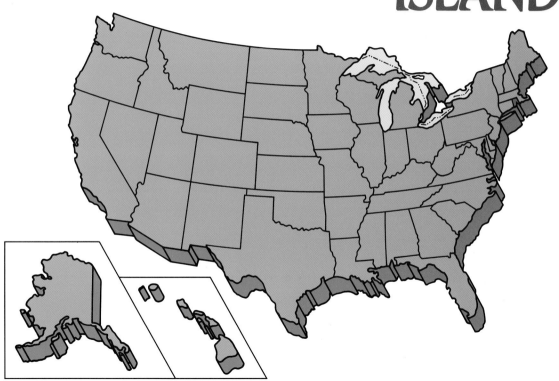

RHODE ISLAND

J. F. Warner

EAU CLAIRE DISTRICT LIBRARY

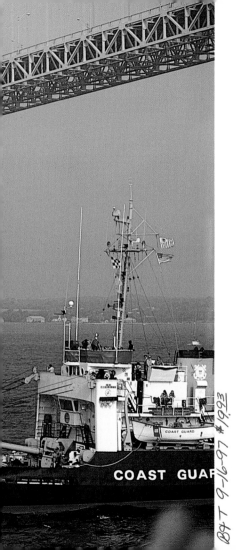

Lerner Publications Company

T 111461

B+T 9-16-97 #1993

Copyright © 1993 by Lerner Publications Company, Minneapolis, Minnesota

All rights reserved. International copyright secured. No part of this book may be reproduced, stored in a retrieval system, or transmitted in any form or by any means—electronic, mechanical, photocopying, recording, or otherwise—without the prior written permission of Lerner Publications Company, except for the inclusion of brief quotations in an acknowledged review.

LIBRARY OF CONGRESS
CATALOGING-IN-PUBLICATION DATA
Warner, J. F.
    Rhode Island / J. F. Warner
        p.   cm. — (Hello USA)
    Includes index.
    Summary: An introduction to the geography, history, economy, people, environmental issues, and interesting sites of Rhode Island.
        ISBN 0-8225-2731-6 (lib. bdg.)
    1. Rhode Island—Juvenile literature.
    [1. Rhode Island.] I. Title. II. Series.
    F79.3.W37   1992
    974.5—dc20   91-40640
                                                CIP
                                                 AC

Cover photograph courtesy of Rhode Island Division of Agriculture.

The glossary on page 69 gives definitions of words shown in **bold type** in the text.

Manufactured in the United States of America

1   2   3   4   5   6   98   97   96   95   94   93

 This book is printed on acid-free, recyclable paper.

CONTENTS

Did You Know . . . ?

❑ Rhode Island, the nation's smallest state, has the longest official name—State of Rhode Island and Providence Plantations.

❑ Some of the tuna fish caught in the waters off Rhode Island weigh nearly 1,000 pounds (454 kilograms). That's enough to make 20,000 tuna fish sandwiches!

❑ About 220 Rhode Islands could fit into the state of Texas. Because of its small size, Rhode Island is sometimes called Little Rhody.

❏ Rhode Island's state bird is a chicken. The Rhode Island Red was first bred in Little Compton, Rhode Island, in 1854. The bird's plentiful eggs and tasty meat made it the chicken of choice for U.S. poultry farmers.

❏ Rhode Island claims the nation's first public roller-skating rink (1866), first golf course (1890), and first automobile parade (1899).

Rhode Island Red

A Trip Around the State

"Good things come in small packages." Whoever thought up that old saying could well have had Rhode Island in mind. Rhode Island is just 59 miles (95 kilometers) long and 40 miles (65 km) wide. A person can take an unhurried tour of the entire state in a single day! Travelers who do will discover a greater variety of scenery than they might expect to find in the smallest state in the country.

There are rivers, lakes and ponds, farms and forests, rolling hills, sandy beaches, bustling cities, and quiet villages. And Narragansett Bay is no more than a 30-minute drive from anywhere in the state. Narragansett Bay, an inlet of the Atlantic Ocean, is sprinkled with islands of many sizes and descriptions.

9

Because it has about 400 miles (640 km) of coastline, Rhode Island is sometimes called the Ocean State.

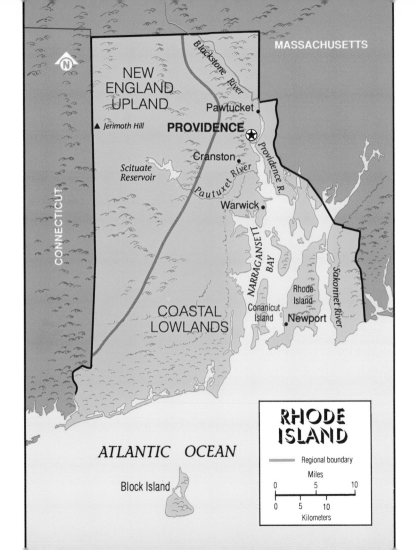

MASSACHUSETTS

NEW ENGLAND UPLAND

▲ Jerimoth Hill

Blackstone River

Pawtucket

PROVIDENCE ★

Cranston

Providence R.

Scituate Reservoir

Pautuxet River

Warwick

CONNECTICUT

NARRAGANSETT BAY

Rhode Island

Conanicut Island

Sakonnet River

Newport

COASTAL LOWLANDS

ATLANTIC OCEAN

Block Island

RHODE ISLAND

━━━ Regional boundary

Miles
0   5   10

0   5   10
Kilometers

Rhode Island is one of six states in a region of the northeastern United States known as New England. Tucked into the southeastern corner of New England, Rhode Island is bordered on the north and east by Massachusetts and on the west by Connecticut. The waters of the Atlantic Ocean form Rhode Island's southern boundary.

Rhode Island has two main land regions. They are the Coastal Lowlands in the south and east and the New England Upland in the northwest. Both regions were formed by the **glaciers** that covered much of North America thousands of years ago. As these huge blocks of ice and snow crept down from the north, they carried sand and clay with them. When the glaciers finally melted, they left ridges of dirt and rock, called **moraines.**

By far the larger of the two regions, the Coastal Lowlands covers nearly two-thirds of Rhode Island. The region includes much of the mainland, all the islands in Narragansett Bay, and the lands bordering Massachusetts. Rhode Island's largest cities and most of its people are found in the Coastal Lowlands.

Block Island, located south of the mainland in the Atlantic Ocean, is part of Rhode Island's Coastal Lowlands region.

EAU CLAIRE DISTRICT

The shores of Rhode Island's lowlands are marked by sandy beaches and numerous salt ponds and **lagoons**. Rocky cliffs overlook Narragansett Bay from the coast and from many of its islands.

The Coastal Lowlands rises in height until it meets the New England Upland. The upland begins where the land reaches a height of 200 feet (60 meters) above sea level and continues on up to 812 feet (247 m) at Jerimoth Hill—the highest point in the state. Small towns, farms, and forests dot the New England Upland.

Spring Lake in northern Rhode Island is one of many lakes scattered throughout the New England Upland.

EAU CLAIRE DISTRICT LIBRARY

Rhode Island's largest inland body of water is Scituate Reservoir. This **reservoir,** or artificial lake, was made to store water for the capital city of Providence. The city and its surrounding communities get their water through a series of underground pipes leading from Scituate to individual homes and businesses.

The Blackstone, the Sakonnet, and the Pawtucket are among the state's chief rivers. The Blackstone River begins in northeastern Rhode Island and flows southward. It is renamed the Seekonk and then the

Providence River before reaching Narragansett Bay. The Sakonnet River is actually a saltwater arm of the bay. The Pawtucket River flows from Scituate Reservoir into the Providence River.

Despite Rhode Island's northern location, the state's climate is mild. January temperatures average 29° F (-2° C). In July temperatures average 71° F (22° C). **Precipitation** (rain and melted snow) averages 44 inches (112 centimeters) a year. More than half of this moisture falls in the form of snow, mostly in the New England Upland.

15

Hurricanes damage coastal areas, including roads.

Apple blossoms

If Rhode Island is affected most by any one type of natural disaster, it is hurricanes. Over the years, the state has been hit many times by the strong winds and heavy rains created by these destructive coastal storms. Hurricanes usually occur in August or September.

More than half of Rhode Island is forested, and trees are one of the state's most valuable resources. Some of the most common trees include ash, birch, cedar, oak, pine, and, of course, the state's official tree—the red maple. Wild plants such as dogwoods, mountain laurels, rhododendrons, and violets add delicate touches of color in the spring.

Numerous streams and ponds help support many kinds of wildlife in the state's forests. Deer, foxes, and mink, along with game birds such as partridge, pheasant, wild turkeys, and quail abound.

Red fox

The Narraganset Indians lived in what is now Rhode Island. They fished Narragansett Bay *(left)* for flounder and shellfish. During a special ceremony, the Indians smoked tobacco in a long, feathered pipe *(inset)*.

Rhode Island's Story

As long as 10,000 years ago, people were living in the part of North America now known as New England. Little is known about these early Native Americans. We do know that by the 1500s, 30,000 to 40,000 descendants of the early Indians were living in five tribes located throughout what is now Rhode Island.

The largest and most powerful of these tribes was the Narraganset, who made up at least half of the area's population. They shared the area with the Wampanoag, Nipmuc, Niantic, and Pequots.

These Native Americans were farmers, hunters, and fishers. They lived in wigwams—homes supported by poles covered with tree bark or animal skins. The Indians used beads as money. They passed stories and knowledge from generation to generation by word of mouth.

Each village had a judge who sentenced criminals according to a fixed set of rules. Tribe members liked to compete in running and swimming, and they played a game something like American football.

No one knows for sure which group of Europeans first visited what is now Rhode Island. Some people believe it was the Vikings, from Scandinavia. Others say the Portuguese. In any event, the first real evidence comes from the writings of Giovanni da Verrazano. He was an Italian explorer who explored the Narragansett Bay area in 1524 and described it in his diary.

No one knows exactly when the Old Stone Mill was built or even who built it. Some people think it was constructed more than a thousand years ago by the Vikings. Others say the structure dates from the early 1600s.

Verrazano was later followed by Adriaen Block, a Dutch sailor who arrived in the bay in 1614. Neither Verrazano nor Block had planned to bring settlers from his home country to live near Narragansett Bay. That feat was left for the British to accomplish.

In Great Britain in the early 1600s, the Church of England and the government were practically one and the same. Those who did not follow the laws of the church were punished severely by the government. Sometimes they were thrown in jail or even put to death. Some people fled Great Britain to practice the religion of their choice.

The Puritans, a religious group that wanted to "purify" the Church of England, left Britain in

Adriaen Block explored Rhode Island's coast in the early 1600s. Block Island is named after him.

the early 1600s. They sailed across the Atlantic Ocean to North America, where they founded the Massachusetts Bay Colony in what is now Massachusetts.

Roger Williams

In the **colony**, residents, or colonists, still thought of themselves as British citizens and obeyed the orders of the king of Britain. But in their faraway colony, the Puritans could change the rules of the church without being punished.

Roger Williams, a Puritan minister, left England in 1630 with his wife and newborn daughter. They sailed to Boston, center of the Massachusetts Bay Colony, with high hopes of experiencing true freedom of religion. Their hopes were soon dashed, however. The Puritans had their religious freedom but demanded that everyone who joined the colony follow the beliefs of the Puritan church.

Williams's religious views differed somewhat from those of the

Puritans in Massachusetts. He fled the colony soon after learning that the Puritans were planning to send him back to Britain because of his beliefs.

Williams headed south to a spot near Narragansett Bay. There, in 1636, he founded the city of Providence on land given to him by the Narraganset, whom he had befriended. Then he invited any and all to join him in his new city. Baptists, Quakers, Jews, people of no religion—all were welcome.

In Providence people could worship in the church of their choice—a freedom unheard of in the Massachusetts Bay Colony or in Great Britain.

In 1643, 40 armed soldiers from Massachusetts surrounded the home of Samuel Gorton in Warwick, a town near Providence. Gorton's crime was that he set foot in Massachusetts after having been banned from the colony a few years earlier for his religious beliefs. The soldiers took Gorton to Massachusetts, where he was sentenced to six months hard labor before being allowed to return to Warwick.

Eventually, new settlements grew up around Providence. The Puritans in Massachusetts Bay tried to gain control of these new settlements. Under the Puritans, the religious freedoms enjoyed by the settlers would be lost. Alarmed, Roger Williams set sail for Britain to convince King Charles I to stop the Puritans.

In 1644 the king gave Williams a **charter,** or written permission, to establish the Providence Plantations in Narragansett Bay. With this charter, Providence and its nearby plantations, or settlements, became an official colony of Great Britain.

The new colony was now an equal of Massachusetts Bay and was protected by the king. The Puritans would not threaten a chartered colony of the powerful king. So Williams and the others were free to worship as they pleased.

The Road to Rhode

In 1663 a second charter gave the colony a new name—the Colony of Rhode Island and Providence Plantations. The colonists soon shortened it to, simply, Rhode Island. Rhode Island was the name of Narragansett Bay's largest island, which up until the mid-1600s had been called Aquidneck. (To avoid confusion, some people still say Aquidneck when referring to the island of Rhode Island.)

No one is quite sure where the name Rhode Island comes from. Some people credit Giovanni da Verrazano, who wrote in 1524 that the island reminded him of the Greek island of Rhodes, in the Aegean Sea. Others believe that the Dutch sailor Adriaen Block, noting the red earth along the island's shoreline, called the place *Roodt Eylandt,* which means "red island" in Dutch.

Meanwhile, more people began leaving Britain to live in North America. Like Williams, some of these settlers were looking for a place to practice their religion. Others wanted to farm or to trade with the Indians. The newcomers established more colonies along the coast. Colonies in what is now the northeastern United States became known as New England.

As more and more people sailed the ocean to settle in New England and the other colonies, Native

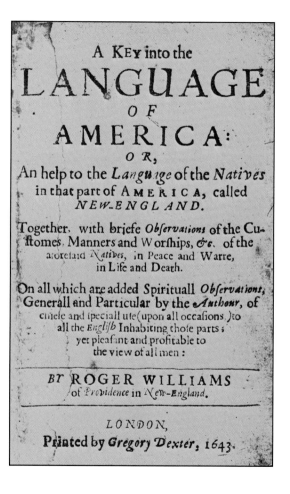

A KEY into the
LANGUAGE
OF
AMERICA:
OR,
An help to the *Language* of the *Natives* in that part of AMERICA, called NEW-ENGLAND.

Together, with briefe *Observations* of the Cuftomes, Manners and Worships, &c. of the aforefaid *Natives*, in Peace and Warre, in Life and Death.

On all which are added Spirituall *Observations*, Generall and Particular by the *Authour*, of chiefe and fpeciall ufe (upon all occafions) to all the *English* Inhabiting thofe parts; yet pleafant and profitable to the view of all men:

BY ROGER WILLIAMS
of Providence in *New-England.*

LONDON,
Printed by *Gregory Dexter*, 1643.

Roger Williams learned how to speak the Narraganset language and even wrote a book about it—*A Key into the Language of America.* Unlike most settlers, Williams treated Native Americans as equals.

Americans became angry. The colonists were not interested in sharing the land. Often, they simply took it from the Indians to build homes and to raise crops.

In 1675 Metacomet (called King Philip by the colonists), chief of the Wampanoag, went to war against the New England colonists. Metacomet and his supporters wanted to regain their homeland. The major battle of King Philip's War was fought in Rhode Island. On December 19, 1675, about 500 Wampanoag and Narraganset were killed in the Great Swamp Fight near Kingston, Rhode Island. Many of the Indians who survived were sold into slavery.

Less than a year after the war began, Metacomet was tracked down and slain. Without Metacomet's leadership, Native Americans in the New England colonies became almost powerless. The Indians lost King Philip's War in 1678. In Rhode Island, the Native Americans still left were given a small plot of land on which to live.

In 1676 Metacomet was killed by an Indian who fought on the side of the settlers.

◄From Rum to Riches►

In the 1700s, the colonists of Rhode Island dabbled in what became known as the triangular trade and soon discovered wealth beyond anyone's imagination.

For Rhode Islanders, the triangular trade involved three ports and three cargoes. It began in Newport, where merchant ships were loaded with kegs of rum. The rum was shipped to West Africa, where the liquor was traded for Africans. The Africans were shipped to the West Indies to be sold into slavery in exchange for molasses, sugar, and money.

Then came the last stage and the completion of the triangle. The ships returned to the colonies, where the remaining Africans were sold into slavery. The sugar and molasses from the West Indies were used to make more rum, which was used to buy more African slaves.

The trade went on and on, and the colonists made huge profits. At the time, the cost of making rum was about 25 cents a gallon. Merchants could buy slaves in Africa for about 200 gallons of rum, or $50. Slaves sold in the colonies for up to $400 each.

Narragansett Pacer

Throughout the 1700s, Rhode Islanders turned more and more to the sea for wealth. Providence, Newport, and Bristol became bustling seaports. Rhode Islanders built vessels for hunting whales. The large sea animals were caught for their blubber, or fat, which was cooked into an oil. The colony's fleet of merchant ships carried milk, cheese, wood, and the Narragansett Pacer—a famous breed of horse—to other parts of the world.

The king wanted Rhode Islanders and other colonists to rely on Great Britain for some of their goods. He decided to make it difficult for colonists to make a profit. He created new taxes and refused to allow the colonists to make certain products, such as iron goods and cloth.

The colonists' dislike for these and other laws led to the beginning of the American Revolution. In 1775 the 13 colonies joined together to fight for the right to make their own laws.

Few battles were fought in Rhode Island during the revolutionary war, but two Rhode Islanders played large roles as leaders of the Continental, or colonial, troops. Esek Hopkins of Providence was commander-in-chief of the Continental navy. Nathanael Greene of Warwick was a respected general in the Continental army.

Esek
Hopkins

Nathanael
Greene

On May 4, 1776, Rhode Island became the first colony to formally declare itself independent of Great Britain. On July 4, 1776, representatives from the colonies approved the Declaration of In-

In 1780 French troops landed in Newport to aid Continental forces throughout the colonies. Without the help of the French, the colonists might have lost the war.

dependence, a letter stating that the colonies were officially free of British rule. With the signing of the Declaration of Independence, the United States of America was born, but the colonists did not actually defeat the British until years later, in 1783.

The former 13 colonies could not become states of the Union until they approved the U.S. Constitution, or listing of the country's laws. Although Rhode Island had been the first colony to declare independence, it was the last to formally approve the Constitution. On May 29, 1790, Rhode Island became the 13th state.

31

Rhode Island's state flag features an anchor surrounded by 13 stars. The anchor is a symbol of hope, the state's motto, and the stars represent the original 13 colonies.

At about the same time, Moses Brown, a wealthy merchant from Providence, and Samuel Slater, a British textile worker, met in Pawtucket, Rhode Island. Slater had the plans to an invention that would change the United States forever.

In Pawtucket the two men built the country's first waterpowered cotton mill. This event marked the beginning of the **Industrial Revolution** in the United States. For the first time in U.S. history, people left their spinning wheels at home and went to work in factories, where products such as cloth could be made much faster. Since working the machinery required little practice, even people unskilled in the making of cloth could work in the factory.

By the late 1700s, the British had developed waterpowered machines that produced certain goods quickly and efficiently, spurring industrial growth in Great Britain. Spinning machines for making thread and yarn were among these inventions. To make sure other countries did not profit from these powerful tools, Britain made it illegal to take any machines—or the plans or models to make them—out of the country. Even the people who worked with the machines were not allowed to leave.

Disguised as a farmer, textile worker Samuel Slater escaped and traveled to America. From memory he re-created the waterpowered spinning machines developed by Richard Arkwright in Britain. The machines poured out cotton yarn at speeds faster than Americans had ever seen. Slater opened a cotton mill, or factory, in Pawtucket. Before long, the number of factories using waterpowered machinery had multiplied, and the American Industrial Revolution was born.

Some millworkers had to stand while they worked 14-hour days.

By 1840 the population of Rhode Island was 140,000. Waves of **immigrants**—including children—arrived to work in the many cotton and woolen mills that had been built in the state. First came the Irish, then the French Canadians and Swedes, followed by Poles, Greeks, and Russians. Later came the Portuguese, Chinese, and Italians.

Despite Rhode Island's growth, its government had fallen far behind the times. The charter of 1663, still the supreme law of Rhode Island, awarded voting rights only to male landowners and their eldest sons. In the mid-1800s, less than 40 percent of the state's population had a say in government.

Thomas W. Dorr, a fiery activist, wanted to change the outdated voting law. In 1842 he started what became known as Dorr's Rebellion. Dorr's followers were the

GOVERNOR DORR

GOVERNOR DORR

CIGARS
EXTRA * FINE

In 1842 Thomas Dorr was elected governor of Rhode Island. The election, however, was unofficial, and the state government never recognized Dorr's title.

landless, many of whom were immigrants. Dorr and his supporters wrote a new state constitution that gave more people the right to vote, and then they held their own elections.

Dorr formed an army and tried to take over the state government by force. The rebellion failed, and Dorr left Rhode Island. Some of Dorr's ideas about voting, however, were accepted in a new state constitution passed in 1843.

In the late 1800s, the sea was still important to Rhode Island. The U.S. Navy opened a base in Newport. Whaling, shipbuilding, and fishing flourished. If any industry weakened it was farming. As Rhode Island's population grew, companies bought land from farmers to build housing for millworkers and their families. Many farmers, whose incomes depended on how well their crops did, left their fields to work in the mills for steady wages.

The Naval War College in Newport has been a training center for navy officers since 1884.

The navy's presence in Rhode Island grew. In 1883 the Newport Naval Station began docking large ships in Narragansett Bay's deepwater ports. In 1884 the Naval War College started training students in naval military tactics.

During World War I (1914–1918), shipyards in the bay area built combat boats. During World War II (1939–1945), the navy opened the Quonset Point Naval Air Station, and the entire bay area became a beehive of naval activity.

In the late 1800s and early 1900s, Rhode Island became a fashionable summer vacation place for the rich, many of whom built large mansions along the coast.

A labor shortage during World War II prompted many women to enter the work force for the first time. In Newport, factory workers were needed to make torpedoes.

After the war ended in 1945, the navy remained, but many of the warships were taken to other ports. Wartime industries, such as electronics and plastics, changed the products they made. These types of factories replaced many of the cotton and woolen mills that had moved to the southern states, where the mills were much cheaper to operate.

By the 1960s, the state had begun to encourage people from other states to vacation in Rhode Island, hoping to create jobs in hotels and restaurants. Visitors were able to reach the islands in Narragansett Bay more easily in 1969, when the Newport Bridge was completed. The bridge connects the island of Rhode Island with Conanicut Island.

The Newport Bridge was completed in 1969. It is 2.5 miles (4 km) long.

8,000 B.C. Indians inhabit the area now called Rhode Island

A.D.1524 Giovanni da Verrazano explores Narragansett Bay

1636 Roger Williams founds Providence

1675 Great Swamp Fight

1776 Rhode Island declares independence

1790 American Industrial Revolution begins in Pawtucket; Rhode Island becomes the 13th state

New waves of immigrants in the 1970s and 1980s added to the state's ethnic mix. Puerto Ricans, Colombians, and Southeast Asians settled in the state. This mix of Rhode Islanders enjoys freedom to a degree that would make Roger Williams smile proudly.

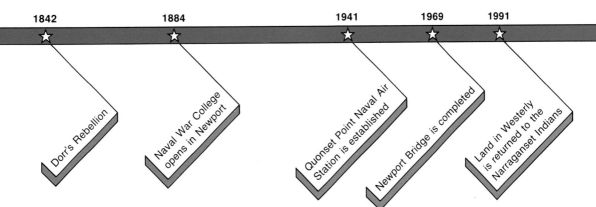

1842 — Dorr's Rebellion

1884 — Naval War College opens in Newport

1941 — Quonset Point Naval Air Station is established

1969 — Newport Bridge is completed

1991 — Land in Westerly is returned to the Narraganset Indians

In 1991, after 259 years, a Rhode Island family returned hundreds of acres of land to the Narraganset Indians. The Crandall family, who could no longer afford to keep the land, wanted to turn it over to people who would preserve the woods and swampland.

41

Tall buildings *(left)* line the business district of Providence, Rhode Island's largest city. Hundreds of people crowd a beach *(facing page)* in Rhode Island in the summertime.

Living and Working in Rhode Island

Living and working in Rhode Island means living and working in an ethnically mixed state. Most of the population can trace their roots back to various countries in Europe. Latinos, African Americans, Asian Americans, and Native Americans make up only 12 percent of the state's one million people.

The few thousand Native Americans in Rhode Island are descendants of the Narraganset and the Wampanoag, who greeted the first European settlers more than 300 years ago.

Living and working in Rhode Island also means being in one of the most crowded states in the nation. For each square mile of land, there are more than 800 persons (300 persons for each sq km). Of the 50 states, only New Jersey is more densely populated.

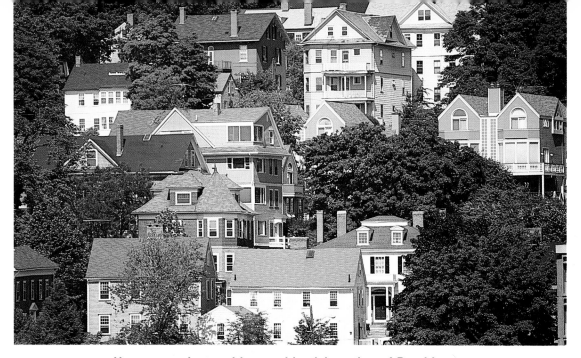

Homes are clustered in a residential section of Providence.

Nearly all Rhode Islanders—close to 90 percent—live in cities. Rhode Island's most populated city is Providence, the capital. Warwick, Cranston, and Pawtucket are other large cities in Rhode Island. All of these cities are near Narragansett Bay.

Much of Providence is a living museum. Many of its parks and gardens, splendid buildings, and gracious homes date back to colonial days. Providence also boasts two world-famous schools—Brown University and the Rhode Island School of Design, each with museums of its own. The city has professional theater groups, an opera, and a ballet company.

Providence is not the only cultural center in Rhode Island. The village of Wickford on the shores of Narragansett Bay holds an art show that draws artists and art lovers from all across the country each year.

A student at the Rhode Island School of Design studies the paintings in the school's Museum of Art.

A Narraganset Indian wears some traditional beadwork.

The town of Matunuck on the Atlantic coast has a summer theater noted for its plays and musicals. In nearby Charlestown, on a **reservation** owned by the Narraganset, Native Americans hold an annual fall festival, where for a week they expose visitors to Narraganset history and customs.

Newport is the home of numerous historical sites. Built in 1747, the Redwood Library is the oldest library still in use in Rhode Island. The Old Stone Mill, a structure some people believe was built by the Vikings, may be more than a thousand years old. Newport also hosts jazz and folk festivals, as well as an international festival of classical music.

Crowds *(above)* **fill the concert grounds of Newport's JVC Jazz Festival, where musicians such as Ray Charles** *(inset, piano player)* **have performed.**

47

Rhode Island takes education seriously. One of the first public schools in the colonies was started in Newport in 1640. Many years later, in 1800, Rhode Island became the first state in the Union to collect taxes to pay for public schools. Nowadays, Rhode Island spends more money per pupil than most other states.

Forests, the ocean, and the bay make Rhode Island a playground for those who love the outdoors. Twenty state parks provide swimming areas, campgrounds, hiking trails, and nature preserves. Sailing, snorkeling, fishing, ice-skating, and skiing can all be enjoyed in season.

Sports fans can watch many competitions throughout the year. Rhode Island has professional tennis and golf matches, sailing races, boat shows, college sports, and an annual marathon. The state also cheers on the Pawtucket Red Sox —the top minor-league team of the professional Boston Red Sox baseball club.

The waters of Rhode Island provide windsurfers with miles of waves.

A pitcher for the Pawtucket Red Sox—
also known as the PawSox—warms up
before a game.

More than half of Rhode Island's
450,000 workers are employed in
service jobs. Service workers have
jobs as teachers, doctors, bankers,
waiters, and bus drivers. Rhode
Islanders who work for the government also have service jobs and
make up another 12 percent of the
work force. The U.S. Navy em-
ploys thousands of service
workers, including engineers and
clerks.

U.S. Navy ships, such as this destroyer *(above),* are docked at Newport Harbor. Rhode Island's crops include Christmas trees *(facing page, left)* and apples *(facing page, right).*

Nearly 30 percent of Rhode Island's workers have jobs in manufacturing. The state is a leader in making jewelry and silverware. Both of these industries are centered in Providence. Rhode Islanders also make machinery, air conditioners, cloth, plastics, electronics, and ships.

Out of all the agricultural goods produced in Rhode Island, shrubs and trees used for landscaping, Christmas trees, sod, and milk make the most money. Some of the sod, which is grown on special farms, is used to cover the playing fields of many sports stadiums in the northeastern United States.

Trollers are boats that slowly tow several long fishing poles through the water.

Rhode Island's fishing fleet has gotten smaller in the past few years, but fishing is still important to the state's economy. One reason for the industry's success is the high price people will pay for seafood. Another is that people around the world want to eat the fish caught in Rhode Island's waters. Tuna, striped bass, and flounder are as likely to be found on menus in Asia and Europe as in New England.

Nets are used to haul in fish and shellfish.

Shellfish such as lobsters, scallops, and quahogs (hard-shell clams) are in demand wherever seafood lovers can be found. Finally, there is the menhaden catch. Menhaden, fish that are usually processed into fish oil or fertilizer, are caught in huge numbers each fall and winter. Ships from places as far away as Russia anchor in Narragansett Bay to buy the menhaden catch off Rhode Island's fishing boats.

Narragansett Bay

Protecting the Environment

Narragansett Bay plays a large role in the lives of Rhode Islanders. The bay is a major source of food, yielding nearly 40 percent of all hard-shell clams eaten in the United States. Fish such as flounder are caught and sold by the ton. Fish and shellfish together bring in close to $1 billion a year for Rhode Island.

55

Sailboats, speedboats, and yachts fill a marina, or dock, in Rhode Island.

The bay earns Rhode Island even more money from tourism and boating. Tourists spend $1.3 *billion* each year docking their boats, eating at restaurants, and shopping at stores on the bay. Another $60 million comes from the sale of pleasure crafts such as speedboats and yachts.

Narragansett Bay is obviously important to Rhode Islanders, but sometimes it is not treated as well as you might expect. For instance, for more than 100 years, untreated sewage—waste carried by water through sinks and toilets—has been dumped into the bay.

Most of the time, sewage is carried with **wastewater** through pipes to a sewage treatment plant. The plant removes solid matter from the wastewater. The plant then treats, or cleans, the wastewater before releasing it into Narragansett Bay.

Not all sewage, however, makes it to the sewage treatment plant. Some of Rhode Island's sewers are very old. They were built in the 1800s when Rhode Island's cities relied on **combined sewers**—that is, sewers that carry both sewage and storm water directly to the bay.

Cities have since added pipes to the combined sewers to channel both wastewater and storm water to treatment plants. But when there is a heavy rain, storm water fills up these pipes and eventually

the treatment plant. When the treatment plant is completely full, any excess wastewater and storm water go untreated. The polluted water overflows straight into the bay, just as it did 100 years ago.

A combined sewer releases sewage and storm water into the bay.

57

NO SHELLFISHING

POLLUTED AREA

Rhode Island Department of
Environmental Management

Whenever sewage
enters the bay, the
government posts
signs warning people
not to fish.

When untreated sewage overflows into the bay, officials must close beaches, fishing grounds, and shellfish beds for weeks—and sometimes months—at a time. The pollution greatly affects areas where fish or shellfish have their young. The damage costs the fishing and tourism industries millions of dollars every year.

Save the Bay, an organization dedicated to cleaning up Narragansett Bay, works with leaders of industry, with government officials, with ordinary citizens, and with schoolchildren. Save the Bay tries to keep people aware of what's happening in Narragansett Bay by sponsoring an annual swim across the bay, ferryboat rides, and educational programs. The group is also trying to force cities to spend the millions of dollars needed to control pollution from combined sewers.

Shellfishers *(left)* in Rhode Island protest against pollution in their workplace—Narragansett Bay. To help educate students, Save the Bay staff members hold **workshops** *(below)* about the importance of marine life in the bay.

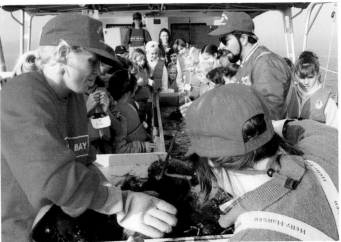

59

Despite the efforts of Save the Bay and other groups, the problems of pollution in Narragansett Bay have not all been solved. About 3.5 billion gallons (13 billion liters) of pollution still end up in the bay each year. Public beaches still close from time to time during the peak summer season. Thousands of acres of rich shellfish beds have been closed to fishers for much of the year because of pollution in the bay.

Many Rhode Islanders are working hard to help the bay. But now it is time for each person to do his or her share by making sure cities are doing all they can to avoid polluting Narragansett Bay. In a state such as Rhode Island—where most people rely on the bay for food, jobs, or leisure—conquering pollution is everyone's business.

A Rhode Island shellfisher digs for quahogs with a bullrake—a long metal pole with a rakelike fixture at one end.

Rhode Island's Famous People

Emma Bugbee (1888–1981) was a journalist who also worked to gain rights for women. In 1911 she became the first female reporter to work in the city-news division of the *New York Herald.* Bugbee lived in Warwick.

Marian Chace (1896–1970) of Providence was a dancer who applied dance as therapy for the mentally ill. In 1965 she founded the American Dance Therapy Association to promote the use of dance as therapy for all types of people.

Princess Red Wing (1896–1986) helped Narraganset Indians in Rhode Island to renew their faith in their culture. Red Wing founded *Red Dawn,* a magazine that explained Narraganset traditions and printed Narraganset legends.

▲ PRINCESS RED WING

ARTISTS & SONGWRITERS

Edward Bannister (1833–1901), who lived in Providence, became one of the first African American artists to gain international fame. His most famous works include a painting entitled *Under the Oaks.*

George M. Cohan (1878–1942) wrote more than 40 plays and musicals, producing and starring in many of them. Cohan, who was from Providence, also wrote many popular songs, such as "Yankee Doodle Boy," "Over There," and "You're a Grand Old Flag."

GEORGE ▶
COHAN

62

Bill Conti (born 1942) wrote the theme songs for the television series "Dynasty," "Falcon Crest," and "Cagney and Lacey." Conti, from Providence, has also written music scores for films, including *North and South, Rocky,* and *The Right Stuff.*

Gilbert Stuart (1755–1828) became famous for the portraits he painted of U.S. presidents and other famous people. His portrait of George Washington appears on the one-dollar bill. Stuart was born in North Kingstown, Rhode Island.

◄ GILBERT STUART

HUGH ► DUFFY

◄ NAPOLEON LAJOIE

BASEBALL PLAYERS

Hugh Duffy (1866–1954) was born in River Point, Rhode Island. During his 68-year baseball career, Duffy participated as player, manager, and executive. In 1945 he was named to the National Baseball Hall of Fame. Duffy still holds the all-time record for the highest single-season batting average (.438 in 1894).

Charles ("Gabby") Hartnett (1900–1972) of Woonsocket was one of baseball's greatest catchers. Because of his rosy complexion and serious expression, Hartnett was nicknamed Old Tomato Face. He was named the National League's Most Valuable Player in 1935.

Napoleon ("Larry") Lajoie (1875–1959) has been called baseball's most graceful infielder. The second baseman from Woonsocket played for Philadelphia and Cleveland. In 1937 he became the sixth player to be elected to the National Baseball Hall of Fame.

BUSINESS LEADERS

Jabez Gorham (1792–1869) of Providence founded Gorham Inc. in 1842. Gorham's was the first company to use machines to plate silver.

Samuel Slater (1768–1835) is considered the founder of the cotton industry in the United States. Born in England, Slater was an apprentice to the inventor of a cotton-spinning machine that could produce thread faster than a spinning wheel. Slater moved to Pawtucket, Rhode Island, reproduced the machine, and became part owner of Slater Mill, the first successful spinning mill in the United States.

◀ SAMUEL SLATER

◀ RUTH BUZZI

▲ NICHOLAS COLASANTO

◀ DAVID HARTMAN

ENTERTAINERS

Ruth Buzzi (born 1936) has appeared on many television shows, including "Laugh-In," "Trapper John, M.D.," and "Alice." The comedian from Westerly has won a Golden Globe Award and is a member of the Rhode Island Hall of Fame.

Nicholas Colasanto (1923–1985) was a television and film actor from Providence. One of the last roles he played was the character of Coach Ernie Pantusso on the long-running television series "Cheers."

David Hartman (born 1935) has worked in television as an actor, host, and producer. He is most commonly associated with ABC's talk show "Good Morning America," which he co-hosted from 1975 to 1987. Hartman is from Pawtucket.

Matilda Sissieretta Joyner Jones (1869–1933) studied music in Providence for many years. In 1892 Jones performed at the White House for President Benjamin Harrison. That same year, Jones became the first African American to sing at New York's Carnegie Hall.

◀ AMBROSE
BURNSIDE

▼ ROBERT GRAY

MATILDA ◀
JONES

◀ IDA LEWIS

EXPLORERS & HEROES

Ambrose Burnside (1824–1881), who lived in Bristol, became governor of Rhode Island after serving as a general for the Union army during the Civil War. Burnside's thick whiskers gave rise to the term *sideburns*.

Robert Gray (1755–1806) was an explorer from Tiverton, Rhode Island. In 1790 he captained the first American ship to sail around the world.

Ida Lewis (1842–1911) began working at the age of 15 as the lighthouse keeper on Lime Rock in Newport Harbor. During her 50 years on the job, Lewis rescued at least 18 people from drowning. Her deeds gained her worldwide fame and a medal from President Ulysses S. Grant.

Sherwood Spring (born 1944), an astronaut, has flown on several space-shuttle voyages, supervising the experiments performed on each mission. Born in Providence, Spring now makes his home in Harmony, Rhode Island.

SHERWOOD ▶
SPRING

65

Facts-at-a-Glance

Nickname: Ocean State
Song: "Rhode Island"
Motto: Hope
Flower: violet
Tree: red maple
Bird: Rhode Island Red
Shellfish: quahog

Population: 1,003,464*
Rank in population, nationwide: 43rd
Area: 1,545 sq mi (4,002 sq km)
Rank in area, nationwide: 50th
Date and ranking of statehood:
    May 29, 1790, the 13th state
Capital: Providence
Major cities (and populations*):
    Providence (160,728), Warwick (85,427),
    Cranston (76,060), Pawtucket (72,644)
U.S. senators: 2
U.S. representatives: 2
Electoral votes: 4

Places to visit: The Breakers mansion in Newport, Slater Mill in Pawtucket, Naval War College Museum in Newport, Old Stone Mill in Newport, Westminster Mall in Providence, Old Narragansett Church in North Kingstown

Annual events: May Breakfasts, statewide (May), Festival of Historic Houses in Providence (June), International Tennis Hall of Fame Championships in Newport (July), Rhode Island Marathon in Newport (Nov.), International Quahog Festival in North Kingstown (Oct.)

*1990 census

66

Natural resources: soil, water, forests, granite, limestone, sandstone, sand and gravel

Agricultural products: shrubs, trees, milk, eggs, poultry

Fishing: clams, flounder, lobster, bluefin tuna, menhaden

Manufactured goods: jewelry and silverware, metal products, electrical equipment

ENDANGERED SPECIES
Mammals—fin whale, humpback whale, right whale
Birds—American bittern, bald eagle, northern harrier, peregrine falcon, yellow-breasted chat, vesper arrow
Reptiles—Atlantic Ridley sea turtle, Atlantic leatherback turtle
Plants—walking fern, slender arrowhead, umbrella grass, small-whorled pogonia, lizard's-tail, dwarf mistletoe, Long's bitter cress, Plymouth gentian, sand plain gerardia, northern blazing star

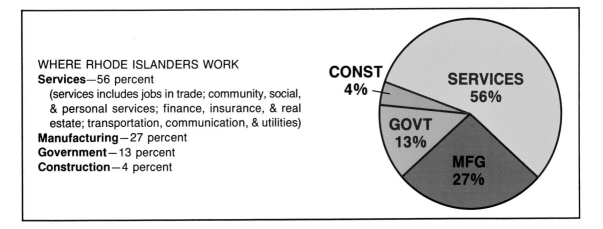

WHERE RHODE ISLANDERS WORK
Services—56 percent
  (services includes jobs in trade; community, social, & personal services; finance, insurance, & real estate; transportation, communication, & utilities)
Manufacturing—27 percent
Government—13 percent
Construction—4 percent

PRONUNCIATION GUIDE

Aquidneck (uh-KWIHD-nehk)

Conanicut (kuh-NAN-ih-kuht)

Narragansett (nar-uh-GANt-suht)

Nipmuc (NIP-muhk)

Pequot (PEE-kwaht)

Sakonnet (suh-KAHN-uht)

Scituate (SIHCH-uh-wuht)

Seekonk (SEE-kahngk)

Verrazano, Giovanni da
　(veh-raht-SAHN-oh,
　joh-VAHN-nee dah)

Wampanoag (wahm-puh-NOH-ag)

Glossary

charter A written statement from the governing power of a territory that guarantees its citizens certain rights and that defines the official boundaries of the territory.

colony A territory ruled by a country some distance away.

combined sewer A system of underground pipes that carries both sewage and storm water.

glacier A large body of ice and snow that moves slowly over land.

immigrant A person who moves into a foreign country and settles there.

Industrial Revolution The change from making products by hand, often at home, to using waterpowered machinery, usually in factories. Powered equipment made it possible for goods to be made quickly, cheaply, and in large quantities. The revolution in the United States began in the late 1700s.

lagoon A shallow lake or pond, especially one that joins a larger body of water.

moraine A mass of sand, gravel, rocks, etc., pushed along or left behind by a glacier.

precipitation Rain, snow, and other forms of moisture that fall to earth.

reservation Public land set aside by the government to be used by Native Americans.

reservoir A place where water is collected and stored for later use.

wastewater Water that carries waste, or sewage, from homes, businesses, and industries.

Index

Acknowledgments:

Maryland Cartographics, Inc., pp. 2-3, 10; © Barbara Laatsch-Hupp / LAATSCH-HUPP PHOTO, pp. 2-3, 37, 50; Toby Schnobrich, p. 6; William J. Weber / Visuals Unlimited, p. 7; Roger Cole / Visuals Unlimited, pp. 8-9, 14-15, 16 (left), 18, 39, 42, 54-55; Jim Simondet, p. 11; R. De Goursey / Visuals Unlimited, p. 12; Jeff Greenberg, pp. 13, 45, 46, 48; Blackstone Valley Tourism Council, Lincoln, Rhode Island, p. 16 (right); Ron Spomer / Visuals Unlimited, p. 17; Rhode Island Historical Society, pp. 18 (inset), 21, 22, 24, 26, 31, 35, 62 (bottom), 65 (bottom left); Library of Congress, p. 23; Doyen Salsig, pp. 28, 68; Independent Picture Service, p. 29, 65 (top); *Dictionary of American Portraits,* pp. 30 (top), 63 (top, center, bottom), 64 (top), 65 (center left, center right); Independence National Historical Park Collection, p. 30 (bottom); Slater Mill Historic Site, Pawtucket, Rhode Island, pp. 33, 34; From the Collection of the Newport Historical Society (P133), p. 36; From the Collection of the Newport Historical Society (P164), p. 38; Thomas P. Benincas, Jr., p. 41; Steve Wright, p. 43; Root Resources, p. 44; Newport Convention & Visitors Bureau, pp. 20, 47 (top and bottom); Stephen Cloutier, Pawtucket Red Sox, p. 49; Rhode Island Division of Agriculture, pp. 51 (left and right); © Gerry Lemmo, p. 52; Erwin C. "Bud" Nielsen, Tucson, AZ, p. 53; © Joseph L. Fontenot / Visuals Unlimited, p. 56; Jamal Kadri, Save the Bay, pp. 57, 58, 61; Save the Bay, p. 59 (top and bottom); Bruce Eastman, R.I. Shellfisherman's Association, p. 60; Providence Journal-Bulletin, p. 62 (top); Hollywood Book & Poster, Inc., p. 64 (center left, center right, bottom); NASA, p. 65 (bottom right); Jean Matheny, p. 66; C. Browning / Rhode Island Division of Tourism, p. 71.